Tiny Acts of Discipline

GYM DAYS

Tiny Acts of Discipline

GYM DAYS

Kylie Leane

PUBLISHER
Kylie Margaret Leane
kylieleane.com

COVER ART/DESIGN/ILLUSTRATIONS
Kylie Leane

Tea & Whiskers: Pocketbooks
Tiny Acts of Discipline - Gym Days

Paperback Edition / March 2026 Kylie Leane
ISBN: 978-0-6451032-5-0

PRINTED IN AUSTRALIA

For information address:
authorkylieleane@gmail.com

Kylie's Blog can be found online at:
teaandwhiskers.com

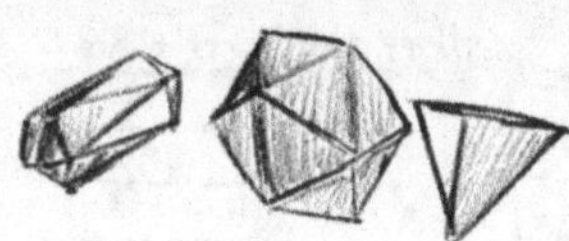

My name is Kylie Leane, gym girl and fibro-warrior.

Living with chronic pain, I've slowly come to understand that discipline is born from tiny acts of consistency, repeated gently over time.
This can be especially difficult when pain blurs the days together and progress feels invisible.

That is why this little pockerbook exists.

It isn't only for those living with chronic pain, but for anyone wanting to record small victories in analog to honour quiet mornings at the gym, or simply to be proud of drinking water at least once in the day

Life can feel overwhelming.

Sometimes all we need is one tiny act to move ourselves forward.

♡ Kylie

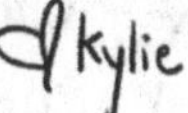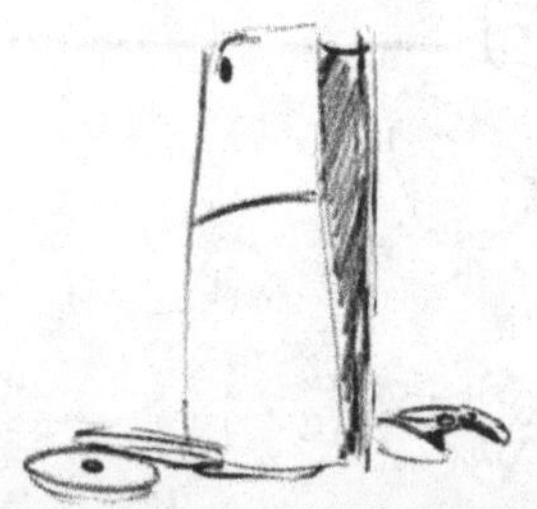

Date _______________

Motivation

Workout Nutrition
____
____
____
____

Workout

Cardio

Exercise	Time/Distance/Speed/Calories

How did today's workout go?

Pain Levels today

Calories _______________

Strength

Exercise	Reps/Wt	Reps/Wt	Reps/Wt	Reps/Wt	Reps/Wt	Reps/Wt

Date

Workout Nutrition

Motivation

Workout

Cardio

Exercise	Time/Distance/Speed/Calories

How did today's workout go?

Pain Levels today

Calories

Strength

Exercise	Reps/Wt	Reps/Wt	Reps/Wt	Reps/Wt	Reps/Wt	Reps/Wt

Date _______________

Motivation

Workout Nutrition _______________

Workout

Cardio

Exercise	Time/Distance/Speed/Calories

How did today's workout go?

Pain Levels today

Calories _______________

Strength

Exercise	Reps/Wt	Reps/Wt	Reps/Wt	Reps/Wt	Reps/Wt	Reps/Wt

Date _______________

Workout Nutrition
____
____
____
____

Motivation

Workout

Cardio

Exercise	Time/Distance/Speed/Calories

How did today's workout go?

Pain Levels today

Calories _______________

Strength

Exercise	Reps/Wt	Reps/Wt	Reps/Wt	Reps/Wt	Reps/Wt	Reps/Wt

Date

Motivation

Workout Nutrition

Workout

Cardio

Exercise	Time/Distance/Speed/Calories

How did today's workout go?

Pain Levels today

Calories

Strength

Exercise	Reps/Wt	Reps/Wt	Reps/Wt	Reps/Wt	Reps/Wt	Reps/Wt

Date

Motivation

Workout Nutrition

Workout

<u>Cardio</u>

Exercise	Time/Distance/Speed/Calories

How did today's workout go?

Pain Levels today

Calories

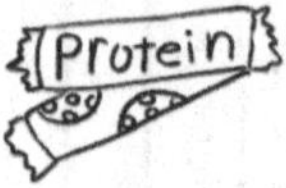

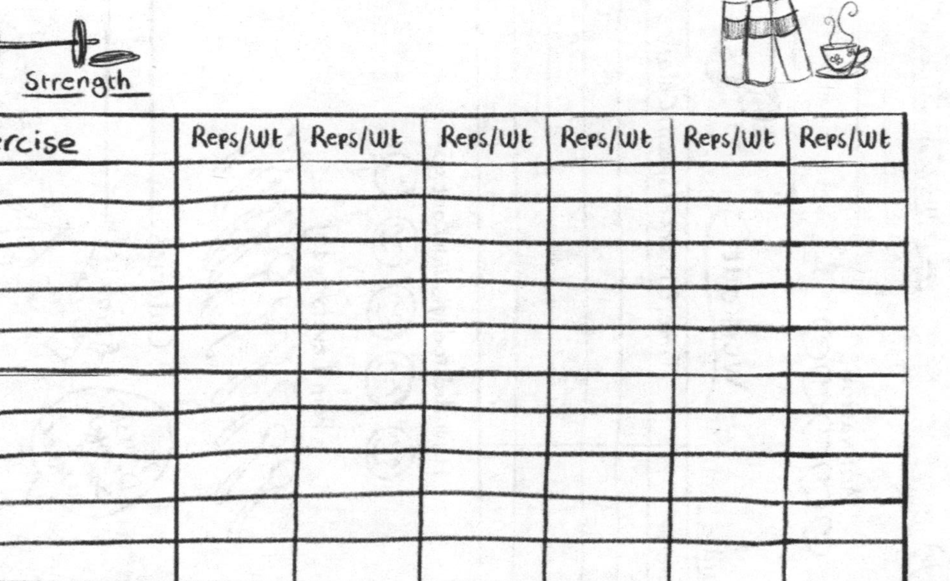

Strength

Exercise	Reps/Wt	Reps/Wt	Reps/Wt	Reps/Wt	Reps/Wt	Reps/Wt

Date

Motivation

Workout Nutrition

Workout

Cardio

Exercise	Time/Distance/Speed/Calories

How did today's workout go?

Pain Levels today

Calories

Thirsty? Drink Some Water

Protein

Strength

Exercise	Reps/Wt	Reps/Wt	Reps/Wt	Reps/Wt	Reps/Wt	Reps/Wt

Exercise	Time/Distance/Speed/Calories

How did today's workout go?

☆ ☆ ☆ ☆ ☆

Pain Levels today

Strength

Exercise	Reps/Wt	Reps/Wt	Reps/Wt	Reps/Wt	Reps/Wt	Reps/Wt

Date

Motivation

Workout Nutrition

Workout

Cardio

Exercise	Time/Distance/Speed/Calories

How did today's workout go?

Pain Levels today

Calories

Strength

Exercise	Reps/Wt	Reps/Wt	Reps/Wt	Reps/Wt	Reps/Wt	Reps/Wt

Date _______________

Motivation

♡ ♡ ♡ ♡ ♡

Workout Nutrition
____
____
____
____

Workout

Cardio

Exercise	Time/Distance/Speed/Calories

How did today's workout go?

😊 😊 😊 😊 😊

Pain Levels today

Calories _______________

Protein _______________

Strength

Exercise	Reps/Wt	Reps/Wt	Reps/Wt	Reps/Wt	Reps/Wt	Reps/Wt

D Date ___________

Workout Nutrition
____
____
____
____

Motivation
♡ ♡ ♡ ♡ ♡

Workout

Cardio

Exercise	Time/Distance/Speed/Calories

How did today's workout go?
☆ ☆ ☆ ☆ ☆

Pain Levels today

Calories ___________

Protein ___________

Strength

Exercise	Reps/Wt	Reps/Wt	Reps/Wt	Reps/Wt	Reps/Wt	Reps/Wt

Date

Motivation

Workout Nutrition

Workout

Cardio

Exercise	Time/Distance/Speed/Calories

How did today's workout go?

Pain Levels today

Calories

Strength

Exercise	Reps/Wt	Reps/Wt	Reps/Wt	Reps/Wt	Reps/Wt	Reps/Wt

Exercise	Time/Distance/Speed/Calories

Strength

Exercise	Reps/Wt	Reps/Wt	Reps/Wt	Reps/Wt	Reps/Wt	Reps/Wt

Date ___________________

Motivation

Workout Nutrition
____
____
____
____

Workout

Cardio

Exercise	Time/Distance/Speed/Calories

How did today's workout go?

☆☆☆☆☆

Pain Levels today

Calories ___________________

{Protein} ___________________

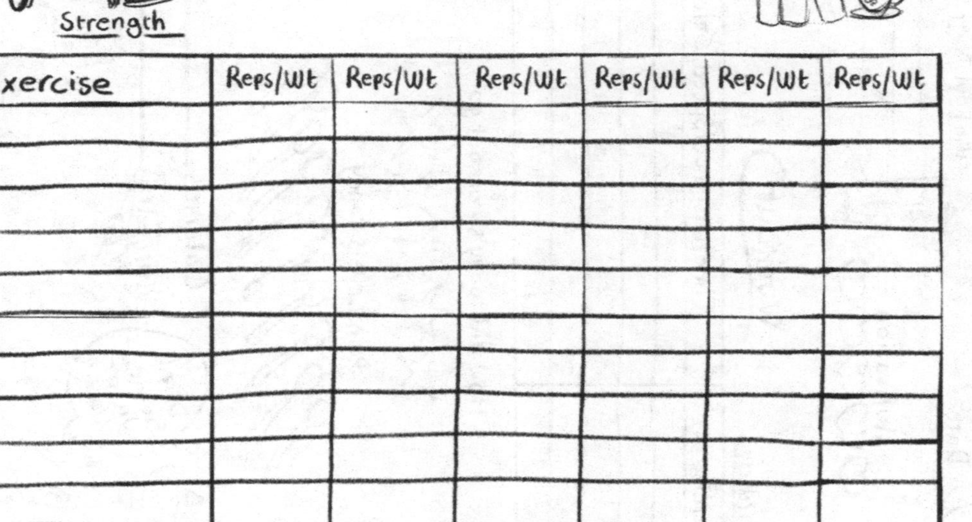

Strength

Exercise	Reps/Wt	Reps/Wt	Reps/Wt	Reps/Wt	Reps/Wt	Reps/Wt

Date ___________

Workout Nutrition
____
____
____
____

Motivation

Workout

Cardio

Exercise	Time/Distance/Speed/Calories

How did today's workout go?

Pain Levels today

Calories ___________

Protein ___________

Strength

Exercise	Reps/Wt	Reps/Wt	Reps/Wt	Reps/Wt	Reps/Wt	Reps/Wt

Date ____________

Motivation

Workout Nutrition
____
____
____
____

Workout

Cardio

Exercise	Time/Distance/Speed/Calories

How did today's workout go?

Pain Levels today

Calories ____________

Protein ____________

Strength

Exercise	Reps/Wt	Reps/Wt	Reps/Wt	Reps/Wt	Reps/Wt	Reps/Wt

Date

Motivation

Workout Nutrition

Workout

Cardio

Exercise	Time/Distance/Speed/Calories

How did today's workout go?

Pain Levels today

Calories

Strength

Exercise	Reps/wt	Reps/wt	Reps/wt	Reps/wt	Reps/wt	Reps/wt

Date _______________

Motivation

Workout Nutrition
____
____
____
____

Workout

Cardio

Exercise	Time/Distance/Speed/Calories

How did today's workout go?

☆ ☆ ☆ ☆ ☆

Pain Levels today

Calories _______________

Strength

Exercise	Reps/wt	Reps/wt	Reps/wt	Reps/wt	Reps/wt	Reps/wt

Date ____________

Motivation

♡ ♡ ♡ ♡ ♡

Workout Nutrition

____
____
____
____

Workout

Cardio

Exercise	Time/Distance/Speed/Calories

How did today's workout go?

☺ ☺ ☺ ☺ ☺

Pain Levels today

Calories ____________

____

Strength

Exercise	Reps/wt	Reps/wt	Reps/wt	Reps/wt	Reps/wt	Reps/wt

Date ___________

Workout Nutrition
____
____
____
____

Motivation

Workout

Cardio

Exercise	Time/Distance/Speed/Calories

How did today's workout go?
☆ ☆ ☆ ☆ ☆

Pain Levels today

Calories ___________

Have I
hydrated
today?

Protein ___________

Strength

Exercise	Reps/Wt	Reps/Wt	Reps/Wt	Reps/Wt	Reps/Wt	Reps/Wt

Date

Motivation

Workout Nutrition

Workout

Cardio

Exercise	Time/Distance/Speed/Calories

How did today's workout go?

Pain Levels today

Calories

Protein

Strength

Exercise	Reps/Wt	Reps/Wt	Reps/Wt	Reps/Wt	Reps/Wt	Reps/Wt

Date

Workout Nutrition

Motivation

Workout

Cardio

Exercise	Time/Distance/Speed/Calories

How did today's workout go?

Pain Levels today

Calories

Strength

Exercise	Reps/Wt	Reps/Wt	Reps/Wt	Reps/Wt	Reps/Wt	Reps/Wt

Date

Motivation

Workout Nutrition

Workout

Cardio

Exercise	Time/Distance/Speed/Calories

How did today's workout go?

Pain Levels today

Calories

Strength

Exercise	Reps/Wt	Reps/Wt	Reps/Wt	Reps/Wt	Reps/Wt	Reps/Wt

Date

Workout Nutrition

Motivation

Workout

Cardio

Exercise	Time/Distance/Speed/Calories

How did today's workout go?

Pain Levels today

Calories

<u>Strength</u>

Exercise	Reps/Wt	Reps/Wt	Reps/Wt	Reps/Wt	Reps/Wt	Reps/Wt

Motivation

Workout Nutrition

Workout

Cardio

Exercise	Time/Distance/Speed/Calories

How did today's workout go?

Pain Levels today

Calories

Strength

Exercise	Reps/Wt	Reps/Wt	Reps/Wt	Reps/Wt	Reps/Wt	Reps/Wt

Date ___________________________

Motivation

Workout Nutrition
____
____
____
____

Workout

Cardio

Exercise	Time/Distance/Speed/Calories

How did today's workout go?

☆☆☆☆☆

Pain Levels today

Calories _______________________

{Protein} _______________________

Strength

Exercise	Reps/Wt	Reps/Wt	Reps/Wt	Reps/Wt	Reps/Wt	Reps/Wt

Date _______________

Motivation

Workout Nutrition
____
____
____
____

Workout

Cardio

Exercise	Time/Distance/Speed/Calories

How did today's workout go?

Pain Levels today

Calories _______________

Strength

Exercise	Reps/Wt	Reps/Wt	Reps/Wt	Reps/Wt	Reps/Wt	Reps/Wt

Date

Motivation

Workout Nutrition

Workout

Cardio

Exercise	Time/Distance/Speed/Calories

How did today's workout go?

Pain Levels today

Calories

Protein

Strength

Exercise	Reps/wt	Reps/wt	Reps/wt	Reps/wt	Reps/wt	Reps/wt

Date

Motivation

Workout Nutrition

Workout

Cardio

Exercise	Time/Distance/Speed/Calories

How did today's workout go?

Pain Levels today

Calories

Protein

Strength

Exercise	Reps/Wt	Reps/Wt	Reps/Wt	Reps/Wt	Reps/Wt	Reps/Wt

Date _______________

Motivation
♡ ♡ ♡ ♡ ♡

Workout Nutrition
____
____
____
____

Workout

Cardio

Exercise	Time/Distance/Speed/Calories

How did today's workout go?

😊 😊 😊 😊 😊

Pain Levels today

Calories _______________

Protein _______________

Strength

Exercise	Reps/Wt	Reps/Wt	Reps/Wt	Reps/Wt	Reps/Wt	Reps/Wt

Reflection